Animals

Kay Davies
and
Wendy Oldfield

Starting Science

Also in paperback:

Floating and Sinking
Sound and Music
Waste

About this book

This book looks at themes within the diversity of animal life and is concerned with both the similarities and differences that can be observed. It is intended to stimulate children's interest in ourselves and the other creatures that share our world.

Animals provides an introduction to science enquiry methods. The activites and investigations are designed to be straightforward but fun, and can be used flexibly to suit the abilities of the children. Through them, the children use a variety of ways to explore the world around them.

The full-page picture in each chapter, with its commentary, may be taken as a focal point for further discussion or as an introduction to the topic. The theme and the animals looked at in each chapter can form a basis for more extensive topic work.

Teachers will find that in using this book, they are reinforcing the other core subjects of language and mathematics. Through its topic approach *Animals* covers aspects of the National Science Curriculum for key stage 1 (levels 1 to 3), for the following Attainment Targets: Exploration of science (AT 1), The variety of life (AT 2), Processes of life (AT 3), Genetics and evolution (AT 4), and Using light and electromagnetic radiation (AT 15).

First published in 1990 by
Wayland (Publishers) Ltd
61 Western Road, Hove
East Sussex, BN3 1JD, England

© Copyright 1990 Wayland (Publishers) Ltd

This edition published in 1991

Typeset by Nicola Taylor, Wayland
Printed in Italy by
    Rotolito Lombarda S.p.A., Milan
Bound in Belgium by Casterman S.A.

British Library Cataloguing in Publication Data
Davies, Kay, *1946 —*
    Animals.
    1. Animals
    I. Title   II. Oldfield, Wendy   III. Series
591

ISBN 0-7502-0281-5

Editor: Cally Chambers

CONTENTS

All the words that first appear in **bold** in the text or illustrations, are explained in the glossary.

Look at all the animals that live in our house.

ANIMAL ALL-SORTS

There are many different kinds of animal in the world.

You will have seen some of them. Can you name any you know?

Find lots of pictures of animals. Put your animals into groups. Use the examples to help you.

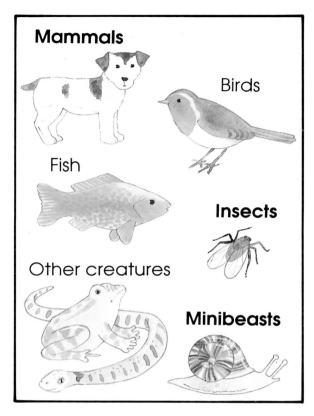

Mammals

Birds

Fish

Insects

Other creatures

Minibeasts

Use your pictures to make an animal scrapbook.

Find out more about your animals.

ME AND MY FAMILY

This boy looks a bit like his parents. They've all got black hair. His mother and father have brown eyes but their son has blue eyes.

What colour are your eyes? Are they the same as the rest of your family?

These twin brothers look exactly alike.

Find photographs of your family. Who do you look like most?

Swap baby pictures of yourself with your friends. Can you guess who each baby is?

The foal looks like its mother and father.

Tadpoles are hatching from some frog's eggs. They will live in the water until their legs have grown.

WHOSE BABY?

Tadpoles are baby frogs. But they do not look like them at all. They change into frogs.

In the spring, collect some **frog spawn** and watch how it changes. Keep it in a glass tank half-filled with pond water. Put in some large stones which show above the water and some pond plants.

Make a tadpole diary. Tick each change you see.

1		Black spot changes shape.	☐
2		Tadpole hatches.	☐
3		Back legs grow.	☐
4		Front legs grow.	☐
5		No tail. Frog hops out.	☐

Dogs have a very good sense of smell. The puppies can smell where the rabbits have been.

Some ducks are swimming on the lake. Some ducks are flying in the air.

The orang-utan can swing through the trees with the help of its long arms.

A LONG REACH

Find some friends. Stand against a wall in a line from shortest to tallest. Now see how high you can reach.

Ask someone to make a mark at the tips of your fingers.

Has the tallest person got the longest reach?

Can you reach to open the door, switch on the light and ring the doorbell?

DON'T EAT ME!

Some birds like to eat butterflies. The spots on the wings of some butterflies can frighten these birds away.

Other butterflies are **camouflaged**. Their colours match the places where they live. They will not be eaten because they cannot be seen.

If you hold a mirror along the dotted line you can see a whole butterfly.

Make your own butterfly.

Fold a large piece of paper in half. Paint half a butterfly on one side. Quickly fold the paper together and press hard. Open it up to see your butterfly.

LOTS OF LEGS

Look under stones, in holes and in the soil for minibeasts like the millipede.

Look at their legs. Do they have lots of legs, eight legs, six legs or no legs at all?

Put them back carefully where you found them.

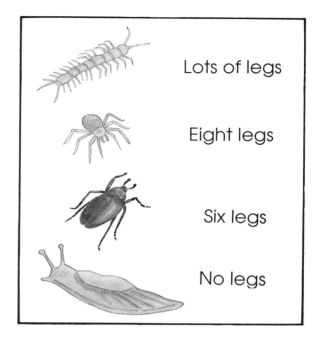

Lots of legs

Eight legs

Six legs

No legs

Make a minibeast clock.

Find two large circles of card and a butterfly pin.

Draw pictures of your minibeasts on one of the cards. Cut a V-shape out of the other card. Pin the two together at the centres.

Slowly wind the clock to see what is hiding in the dark.

SHARP EYES

The cat's eyes look forwards. This helps it to hunt.

The mouse's eyes are on each side of its head. It can look all around. It can see the cat creeping up on it.

Look at animals' eyes. Which animals are hunters and which animals are hunted?

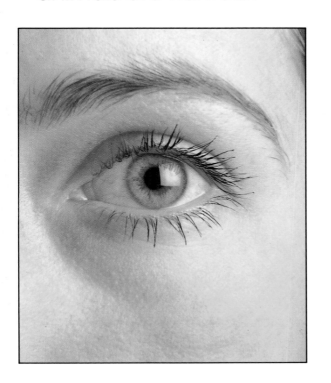

The coloured part of an eye is called the iris. The dark part is called the pupil. The pupil lets light into the eye.

Find out the colours of your friends' eyes. How many are there of each colour?

Owls can see well in the dark. They hunt for food at night.

The spider has spun a sticky trap. It hopes to catch a fly to eat.

A STRONG WEB

People weave traps to catch food. Look at all the fish that have been caught in these nets.

You can weave a strong shape like the net.

Find two pieces of paper which are the same size. Use two different colours.

Cut one into strips. Cut the other like a comb.

Weave your strips of paper in and out of the comb like this.

Can you think of some other ways that we use nets?

The chimpanzee is holding the stick in its hands. It can use the stick to find insects in the wood.

CLEVER HANDS

Chimpanzees' hands are a bit like our own hands. Our thumbs move towards our fingers. We can grip things tightly with our hands.

Can you do all these things?

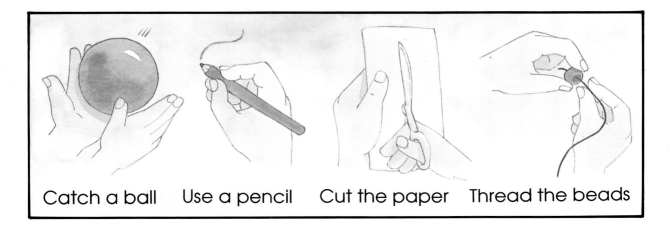

Catch a ball   Use a pencil   Cut the paper   Thread the beads

We can say things like this with our hands.

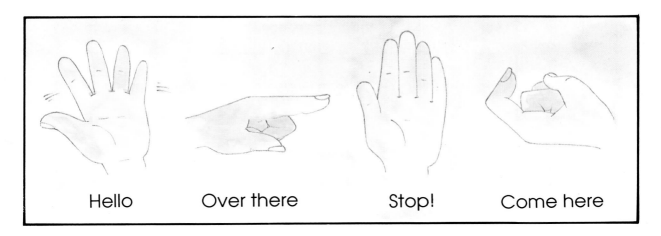

Hello   Over there   Stop!   Come here

How many more can you think of? Talk to your friends with your hands.

GLOSSARY

Camouflaged An animal is camouflaged when it is difficult to see because its colouring and pattern look like its surroundings.

Frog spawn The group of eggs from a frog.

Insects Creatures with six legs.

Mammals Animals that feed their babies with milk.

Minibeasts Insects and other small creatures.

PICTURE ACKNOWLEDGEMENTS

Bruce Coleman Ltd. 7 (Reinhard), 10 (Burton), 13 (Burton), 19 (Purcell), 20 (Kahl), 22 (Clement), 24 (Freeman), 26 (Burton), 27 top (Cubitt), 28 (Davey); Chapel Studios (Zul Mukhida) cover, 4, 5, 6 top, 11, 12 both, 17, 21, 23, 27 bottom; Judith Court 9; Frank Lane Picture Agency 8 (Withers), 15 (Hamblin); Oxford Scientific Films 16 (Gibson), 18; Peter Stiles 14; Topham 6 bottom; ZEFA 25.
Artwork illustrations by Rebecca Archer.
The publishers would also like to thank St. Andrews C.E. School, Hove, East Sussex, for their kind co-operation.

FINDING OUT MORE

Books to read:

A to Z Animals by Beverley Mathias & Ruth Thomson (Franklin Watts, 1989)
All About Baby Animals by Michael Chinery (Kingfisher, 1989)
All About Me by Melanie & Chris Rice (Kingfisher, 1987)
My Class Looks After Pets by Vicky Lee (Franklin Watts, 1988)
My Feather by Jane Mainwaring (A & C Black, 1989)

The following series may also be useful:

Animal Life Stories by Angela Royston (Kingfisher)
Animal Opposites by Mark Carwardine (Wayland)
Baby Animals (Franklin Watts)
First Nature Books by Gunilla Ingves (A & C Black)
First Pets (Franklin Watts)
Keeping Minibeasts (Franklin Watts)
Life Cycles (Wayland)
Look at Animals (Franklin Watts)
Nature Study (Wayland)

INDEX